COUNCIL *on*
FOREIGN
RELATIONS

I0115368

October 2018

Women and the Law
Leveling the Global Economic Playing Field

Rachel Vogelstein, Jamille Bigio, Gayle Tzemach Lemmon,
Meighan Stone, Alexandra Bro, Becky Allen, and Jody Heymann

The Council on Foreign Relations (CFR) is an independent, nonpartisan membership organization, think tank, and publisher dedicated to being a resource for its members, government officials, business executives, journalists, educators and students, civic and religious leaders, and other interested citizens in order to help them better understand the world and the foreign policy choices facing the United States and other countries. Founded in 1921, CFR carries out its mission by maintaining a diverse membership, including special programs to promote interest and develop expertise in the next generation of foreign policy leaders; convening meetings at its headquarters in New York and in Washington, DC, and other cities where senior government officials, members of Congress, global leaders, and prominent thinkers come together with CFR members to discuss and debate major international issues; supporting a Studies Program that fosters independent research, enabling CFR scholars to produce articles, reports, and books and hold roundtables that analyze foreign policy issues and make concrete policy recommendations; publishing *Foreign Affairs*, the preeminent journal of international affairs and U.S. foreign policy; sponsoring Independent Task Forces that produce reports with both findings and policy prescriptions on the most important foreign policy topics; and providing up-to-date information and analysis about world events and American foreign policy on its website, CFR.org.

The Council on Foreign Relations takes no institutional positions on policy issues and has no affiliation with the U.S. government. All views expressed in its publications and on its website are the sole responsibility of the author or authors.

For further information about CFR or this paper, please write to the Council on Foreign Relations, 58 East 68th Street, New York, NY 10065, or call Communications at 212.434.9888. Visit CFR's website, CFR.org.

Copyright © 2018 by the Council on Foreign Relations®, Inc. All rights reserved.

This paper may not be reproduced in whole or in part, in any form beyond the reproduction permitted by Sections 107 and 108 of the U.S. Copyright Law Act (17 U.S.C. Sections 107 and 108) and excerpts by reviewers for the public press, without express written permission from the Council on Foreign Relations.

CONTENTS

INTRODUCTION

Rachel Vogelstein

The connection between women's economic participation and global prosperity is undeniable. Over the past two decades, international organizations and world leaders have increasingly recognized how critical women's economic empowerment and financial inclusion are to economic prosperity and growth. Analyses from the International Monetary Fund (IMF), Organization for Economic Cooperation and Development, the World Bank, and other leading institutions demonstrate the growth potential of women's increased economic participation. UN frameworks such as the Sustainable Development Goals recognize the relationship between economic opportunity for women and development, and include time-bound targets—such as equal access to financial services, natural resources, and technology, and equality in property ownership and inheritance—to advance women's economic participation.

However, despite growing awareness that women's economic empowerment is critical to women, their families, and broader economic prosperity, many countries still legally undermine women's economic participation and undervalue women's work. Of the 189 economies surveyed in the World Bank's *Women, Business and the Law 2018* report, 90 percent have at least one regulation that impedes women's economic opportunities. More than one hundred economies still prevent women from working in certain jobs; fifty-nine economies provide no legal recourse to women who experience sexual harassment in the workplace; and in eighteen countries, men can legally prevent their wives from working outside the home. An array of other legal barriers—from limitations on access to finance to laws restricting women's agency and mobility—prevent women from fully participating in the economy. Even in 2018, the legal landscape for women in the economy fails to reflect the value women's participation adds to economic growth. But change is on the horizon.

Over the last decade, several countries have enacted legal reforms that significantly advance women's rights. Today, all but thirty-two countries legally guarantee gender equality in their constitutions, and a record number of countries now have laws prohibiting discrimination or violence against women. While these gains—rightfully celebrated—show that progress is possible, proposals to eliminate the critical barriers that limit women's economic potential remain absent from mainstream discussions on international and national economic policy, and barriers to female economic enfranchisement persist in every region of the world.

In order to realize the economic potential of 50 percent of the world's population, nations need to do more to level the legal playing field for women. This volume collects in-depth analysis and commentary on legal barriers to women's economic participation, with a focus on five areas in which the greatest obstacles to women's economic participation endure: financial inclusion, identification laws, land rights, workplace discrimination, and family law.

In the opening essay, I make the economic case for eliminating legal barriers that inhibit women's economic participation. Closing gender gaps in the workplace could add an estimated $12 trillion to the global economy. Countries simply cannot afford to waste this economic potential—and governments from Saudi Arabia to Japan are taking notice and enacting policies to promote women's workforce participation.

A web of discriminatory laws impedes women's access to financial services and undermines their capacity to borrow, save, or obtain insurance. In an essay on financial inclusion, Council on Foreign Relations (CFR) Senior Fellow Jamille Bigio highlights how banks stand to benefit economically by ensuring women's access to and use of financial services, by sharing the experience of a Nigerian woman who employed digital tools to save for her daughter's school fees. CFR Senior Fellow Gayle Tzemach Lemmon, reporting on a successful financial inclusion program in Tanzania, explores how education can help women overcome legal and social barriers to opening bank accounts. The economic case for legal reform to promote women's financial inclusion is strong: when women can use financial services without spousal consent and have control over where they live, and when unpaid work is recognized in marital property regimes, gender gaps in financial inclusion are narrowed. Legal reform needs to be a central component of any strategy to advance women's access to and use of savings, credit, and insurance.

One billion people globally still face difficulties in proving their identity, the majority of whom are women and girls, who are consequently disenfranchised on many levels. In an essay on Pakistan, CFR Senior Fellow Meighan Stone explores how the lack of a national identification document can hamper women's ability to participate in all sectors, silencing their political voice and barring their access to the formal economy. In an investigation of two innovative government-led initiatives in South Asia, Stone and Lemmon highlight how governments can take steps to increase women's access to ID cards. Proof of identification is required to vote, go to court, and receive social services. Access to identification is often a precondition to financial inclusion: an identification document is frequently required to open a bank account, apply for credit, and register a business. Gender-based legal differences impede women's ability to obtain national identification documentation in forty-eight countries; some of these obstacles include mandates that women provide additional documentation—and in some cases approval from their fathers or husbands—to receive an ID card or a passport.

Inequality in land ownership is one of the most entrenched social barriers for women. In their essay on property rights, Stone and CFR Research Associate Alexandra Bro explore the effects of land inequality on women and argue that reformers should use international, regional, and national legal frameworks to address persistent disparities. However, in an essay on Afghanistan, Lemmon and former CFR Research Associate Becky Allen demonstrate how legal change is insufficient unless it addresses disparities under customary law. According to the World Bank, close to 40 percent of the world's economies still have at least one legal constraint to women's property rights. This disparity fuels a global gender gap in land ownership, with women comprising less than one-fifth of landholders in sub-Saharan Africa, only 20 percent in Latin America, and as low as 5 percent in the Middle East and North Africa. Equalizing property rights can increase women's economic productivity, improving their income, their ability to take out loans, and the health and education of their families.

Discrimination against women in the workplace remains a global epidemic. As the #MeToo movement gives rise to a global reckoning on sexual harassment, Jody Heymann, dean of the Fielding School of Public Health at the University of California, Los Angeles, and I review the absence of legal protections against this scourge, which can push women out of the formal workforce. Other types of discriminatory workplace laws also hinder women's abilities to rise to leadership positions or even get jobs in certain sectors, as Bigio finds in her essay on

Nigeria's manufacturing industry. Today, 104 economies restrict the kind of jobs that women can hold. Fifty-nine economies have no legal prohibition against sexual harassment in the workplace. Policies that make it difficult for women to remain in the labor force after having children impede their ability to participate in the economy. And in 2018, only 40 percent of economies out of 189 surveyed by the World Bank mandate equal pay. These laws and policies that permit discrimination in the workplace leave women without recourse to address pervasive behaviors that can limit their professional opportunities, thereby short-changing entire economies.

Family law, personal status codes, and deeply rooted social and cultural practices can undermine women's ability to work and contribute to the global economy. In an essay on unpaid care work, Lemmon reviews how social factors such as women's care responsibilities contribute to the global gender gap in workforce participation and highlights how childcare can boost women's paid employment. In a piece on violence against women in Pakistan, Stone illuminates how sexual assault, domestic violence, and other gender-based crimes deter women from pursuing careers in nontraditional fields. Numerous other family law restrictions—such as requirements for familial male permission to seek employment, own a business, control property, petition the courts, or make travel decisions—inhibit women's financial inclusion and economic freedom. Laws that govern marital relations have secondary effects on women's economic empowerment: for example, even though nearly one in three women has experienced physical or sexual violence from an intimate partner—which can undermine economic independence—women in thirty-six countries still have no legal protection against domestic violence whatsoever.

POLICY RECOMMENDATIONS

These essays all suggest that legal reform is a critical step toward boosting women's participation in the global economy. Compelling research demonstrates a substantial link between stronger legal rights and improved development outcomes for women, their families, and their countries. To maximize returns on investment in economic development, the United States should work with other nations to eradicate legal gender inequalities and level the economic playing field for women.

The United States should promote legal and policy reform to advance women's economic participation through its bilateral and multilateral relations. For instance, when negotiating investment treaties and trade agreements, officials should include stipulations to increase women's economic participation and legal equality. Models include the 2017 Canada-Chile Trade Agreement, the first Group of Twenty agreement to include a chapter on gender equality. In addition, the United States should tie bilateral development assistance to progress on women's economic empowerment, building on the Millennium Challenge Corporation (MCC) model, which evaluates the legal position of women in a country when making decisions about whether to provide assistance. The MCC model should be expanded to all U.S. foreign assistance programs to guarantee maximum returns on U.S. investments in women's economic development.

The United States also should use its influence on the multilateral stage to help eliminate legal barriers to women's economic inclusion, building on its leadership of the landmark Asia-Pacific Economic Cooperation (APEC) Declaration on Women in the Economy, by spearheading similar efforts in other regional organizations and leading the way for countries to eliminate obstacles to women's participation. To draw international attention to the persistent legal barriers that continue to impede women's economic opportunity and broader economic growth, the U.S. Treasury and State Departments could start by releasing an annual ranking of countries, modeled on the State Department's Trafficking in Persons Report. This low-cost initiative would raise awareness, create competition, incentivize country-level reforms, and reflect the growing interest among Congress members in promoting women's economic empowerment globally. International organizations also have an important role to play. The United Nations has already pledged its support for women's legal equality in Sustainable Development Goal 5, which calls on member states to achieve gender equality and to adopt and strengthen policies and legislation for the promotion of gender equality and the empowerment of all women and girls. The United Nations should report annually on the progress of member states toward this goal and increase financial resources for gender equality. Multilateral economic institutions should also prioritize legal and policy reform regarding women. The IMF should extend its successful pilot program, which includes appraisals of legal equality in the review processes of twenty countries receiving IMF loans, to all recipient countries. This approach should become standard practice at other multilateral financial institutions as well, starting with regional and subregional development banks, including the African Development Bank, Asian Development Bank, and Inter-American Development Bank.

As this collection of case studies shows, the gains from ensuring that women everywhere have the right to compete fairly in the economy are significant and achievable. Nothing less than humanity's collective prosperity and stability are at stake.

Let Women Work: The Economic Case for Feminism

Rachel Vogelstein

In June, Saudi Arabia will make it legal for women to drive, marking the end of one of the world's most conspicuous examples of gender discrimination.[1] The ban's removal has been rightly hailed as a victory in a country that sysematically limits women's freedoms. But for Saudi officials, this policy reversal has more to do with economics than concern for women's rights. In recent years, even culturally conservative countries such as the Gulf kingdom have begun to recognize that they cannot get ahead if they leave half of their human capital behind.

Women's advocates have long championed gender parity as a moral issue. But in the modern global economy, eliminating obstacles to women's economic participation is also a strategic imperative. A growing body of evidence confirms the positive relationship between women's participation in the labor force and overall growth. In 2013, the Organization for Economic Cooperation and Development (OECD) concluded that a more gender-balanced economy could boost gross domestic product (GDP) by an estimated 12 percent in OECD countries.[2] The International Monetary Fund (IMF) has made similar predictions for non-OECD countries, projecting that greater female economic participation would bring GDP gains of about 12 percent in the United Arab Emirates and 34 percent in Egypt. All told, according to a 2015 report by the McKinsey Global Institute, closing gender gaps in the workplace could add an estimated $12 trillion to global GDP by 2025.[3]

This essay was originally published in *Foreign Affairs*. See Rachel Vogelstein, "Let Women Work: The Economic Case for Feminism," *Foreign Affairs* 97, no. 1 (January/February 2018): 118–124, http://foreignaffairs.com/articles/2017-12-12/let-women-work.

Yet legal barriers to female economic enfranchisement persist in every region of the world, in both developed and developing economies. According to the World Bank, women face gender-based job restrictions in 155 countries, including limitations on property ownership, spousal consent requirements for employment, and laws that prevent them from signing contracts or accessing credit. In many nations, women are still barred from traditionally male jobs or face limits on the number of hours they can work. In Russia, women cannot seek employment in 456 specific occupations, from woodworking to driving a subway. Argentina prohibits women from entering "dangerous" careers, such as in mining, manufacturing flammable materials, and distilling alcohol. French law prevents women from holding jobs that require carrying 25 kilograms (about 55 pounds). In Pakistan, women cannot clean or adjust machinery.

Many economists and analysts are understandably skeptical about the potential for change. After all, deeply embedded cultural norms underpin these discriminatory legal systems. But there is reason to be hopeful. Recognizing the economic imperative, leaders across the globe are pushing for reform. In the last two years alone, 65 countries enacted almost 100 legal changes to increase women's economic opportunities.

"Fully unleashing the power of women in our economy will create tremendous value but also bring much-needed peace, stability, and prosperity to many regions," Ivanka Trump, an adviser to her father, U.S. President Donald Trump, said at a women's entrepreneurship forum in October. Progress, however, will require more than lofty rhetoric. To make real strides in unshackling women's economic potential, the United States will have to use its international clout and foreign aid budget to drive legal reform, not just at home but also in countries across the globe where women cannot fully engage in the economy.

MOMENTUM FOR REFORM

The economic case for eliminating restrictions on women's economic participation is clear.[4] In Saudi Arabia, for example, women earn more than half of all college and graduate degrees but compose only about 20 percent of the labor force. This means that the economic potential of nearly a third of the population remains untapped. As the Saudi economy struggles to cope with low oil prices, increasing female workforce participation has become part of Crown Prince Mohammed bin Salman's ambitious economic modernization effort, known as Saudi Vision 2030.[5] Lifting the driving ban shows that the country is serious about changing the status quo, although many other laws continue to circumscribe the rights of women in the Gulf kingdom.

Even in countries that have far fewer stark gender disparities than Saudi Arabia, leaders have sought to spur economic growth by making it easier for women to participate. In the 1990s, Canadian lawmakers eliminated the so-called marriage penalty, the product of a tax code that had depressed the incomes of secondary earners by requiring couples to pay higher rates in comparison to single taxpayers. In Japan, Prime Minister Shinzo Abe's "womenomics" agenda has put female workers at the center of the country's growth strategy by increasing child-care benefits and incentivizing family-friendly workplace reforms.[6] And in Bangladesh, cabinet ministers are seeking to advance economic development by increasing the share of women in the workplace through infrastructure initiatives, such as bringing electricity to rural areas. These projects reduce the burden of unpaid labor by making household work less time consuming, thereby freeing up time for paid work outside the home.

Countries that have pursued such reforms are already seeing results. In India, after two states changed their succession laws in 1994 to grant women the same right to inherit family property as men, women became more likely to open bank accounts, and their families started to enjoy more financial stability, according to a study conducted by the World Bank in 2010. Similarly, in Ethiopia, since the government eliminated the requirement for a woman to get her husband's consent in order to work outside the home, in 2000, considerably more women have entered the work force and obtained full-time, higher-skilled— and therefore better-paying—jobs. Five years later, women in the three regions where the policy was first implemented were 28 percent more likely to work outside their homes and 33 percent more likely to hold paying jobs than women elsewhere in the country, according to a World Bank analysis. These reforms not only increase women's income but also create a multiplier effect, as women are more likely to invest their earnings in the health, nutrition, and education of their children.

But despite these clear benefits, the pace of change remains far too slow. Saudi women fought for three decades before achieving a repeal of the driving ban. And even after this hard-won victory, the highly restrictive Saudi guardianship system will continue to prevent women from opening a bank account, starting certain businesses, obtaining a passport, or traveling abroad without the permission of a male relative—restrictions that are arguably more significant in limiting their full economic participation than the driving ban.

According to the World Bank, 90 percent of the world's economies still have at least one law on the books that impedes women's economic opportunities.[7] And despite rapid improvements in women's status in other areas—rates of maternal mortality have significantly declined over the last two decades, and the gender gap in primary school education virtually closed over the same time period—women's labor-force participation has actually declined, from 52 percent to 50 percent globally between 1990 and 2016, in part because of the endurance of such legal restrictions.

HELPING WOMEN SUCCEED

Boosting the pace of change should be a priority for U.S. foreign policy—and in recent years, it has been. In 2009, the Obama administration appointed the first-ever U.S. ambassador for global women's issues to lead U.S. efforts on this front. In 2011, the United States hosted the first-ever Asia-Pacific Economic Cooperation ministerial meeting on women in the economy, which led to historic commitments to promote women's inclusion in the workplace, including through legal reform. And in 2014, the United States worked with the Group of Twenty (G20) leaders to set an ambitious target to increase female labor-force participation by 25 percent over the next decade, a goal that would add an estimated 100 million women to the global work force.[8]

The Trump administration should sustain these initiatives and develop new policies that will economically enfranchise women throughout the world. Although the administration has been justifiably criticized for undermining women's rights in health, education, and other areas, it has acknowledged the importance of women's economic participation. In July, Washington put diplomatic and financial resources into the development of the Women Entrepreneurs Finance Initiative (We-Fi), a partnership with the World Bank and other countries that will leverage $1 billion in financing to improve women's access to capital.[9] (This program, which the White House has characterized as the brainchild of Ivanka Trump, in fact expands on a model spearheaded during the Obama administration called the Women Entrepreneurs Opportunity Facility, which continues today and similarly aims to help close the gender gap in access to credit.)

But to truly generate returns on its investment in women's entrepreneurship, the current administration must adopt a more comprehensive approach. Greater access to capital will go only so far if women remain legally prohibited from entering into business relationships or holding positions that are available to men. Indeed, some have criticized We-Fi for failing to take on the systemic legal barriers that impede women's economic participation. Others have questioned the commitment of some of the partner states—including Russia, Saudi Arabia, and the United Arab Emirates—given the gender inequalities enshrined in their laws. Trump's retreat from U.S. leadership on equality and human rights overseas has compounded these doubts. During his May 2017 trip to Saudi Arabia, Trump stated, "We are not here to tell other people how to live, what to do, who to be," at a time when the driving ban, along with various other restrictions on women, remained in full effect. If the administration is serious about advancing women's economic participation globally, it must tackle laws and policies that rig the game against women—and accept the mantle of global leadership, which Trump has spurned.

The United States should start by tying development assistance to progress on women's economic participation, a strategy that would also uphold the administration's commitment to efficient public spending. Some organizations already do this. For example, the Millennium Challenge Corporation (MCC), an aid agency funded by the U.S. government, evaluates the legal position of women in a given country when making decisions about whether to provide assistance, assessing factors including women's ability to sign a contract, register a business, choose where to live, travel freely, serve as the head of a household, and obtain employment without permission. This policy has created "the MCC effect": countries enacting legal reforms in order to attract U.S. aid.[10] In 2006, during negotiations with the MCC, the Parliament of Lesotho ended the practice of giving women the legal status of minors. And in 2007, to secure MCC investment, the Mongolian government enacted property rights reforms that increased the percentage of female landowners and allowed for the collection sex-disaggregated data on land registration to establish a base line for monitoring future progress. The MCC model should be expanded to all U.S. foreign assistance programs to guarantee maximum returns on American investments in women's economic development.

The United States should also encourage similar reforms within multilateral economic institutions. For example, Washington can use its leverage at the IMF to make equal treatment for women in an economy a precondition for obtaining investment and a positive assessment from the fund. The IMF is already running a pilot program that includes appraisals of legal equality in the process of reviewing conditions in 20 countries that receive IMF loans. It should extend that policy to all recipient countries, and this approach should become standard practice at other multilateral financial institutions as well, starting with regional and subregional development banks.

Finally, Washington should draw attention to the persistent legal barriers that continue to impede women's economic opportunity and broader economic growth. The U.S. Treasury and State Departments could start by releasing an annual ranking of countries, modeled on the State Department's Trafficking in Persons Report. This exercise would raise awareness and create competition, incentivizing country-level reforms.

To be sure, legal reforms are just one step on the road to gender parity in the global economy. After all, the reforms must be implemented in the cultural context that gave rise to pervasive discrimination in the first place. And promoting equality on paper will not necessarily improve the situation of women in practice. Genuine progress requires enforcement, which presents its own challenges.

Still, eliminating legal barriers to women's economic participation is essential.[11] Without these reforms, women cannot establish their right to compete in the marketplace. And research shows that legal reforms can precipitate broader societal changes, particularly when combined with community education initiatives. In Senegal, for example, a ban on female genital mutilation, coupled with an information campaign, caused the practice's incidence to drop far more quickly than in comparable nations where it remained legal. By encouraging legal reforms and supporting grass-roots efforts to shift norms, the United States can meaningfully improve women's economic participation.

In advancing this agenda, Washington should not heed the naysayers who claim that promoting gender equality constitutes cultural imperialism. Such assertions ignore the proliferation of domestic groups fighting for women's inclusion around the world, including in Saudi Arabia, where women have been campaigning for the right to drive since 40 courageous women first staged a demonstration in the early 1990s. These critics also overlook the persuasive economic case for female inclusion, which is already galvanizing change across the globe.

At the end of the day, women's economic participation improves societies and drives growth. Leveling the legal playing field is not just a matter of fairness; it is an economic imperative that countries around the world ignore at their own peril. The time has come for Washington to act—and to use its influence to push others to act, as well.

PART I:
FINANCIAL INCLUSION

How a Simple Bank Account Transforms Women's Lives

Jamille Bigio

At her food stall in the largest open-air market in Lagos, Nigeria's commercial capital, Amaka Charles regularly checks her cell phone for her bank account balance. She is saving for her daughter's school fees and dreaming of a loan to expand her business beyond crayfish. Every day, she passes her few dollars of profit to Celestina, the bank agent who daily roams the market to collect vendors' deposits. Charles calls if Celestina is late—she does not want to leave without trading her profit for the "bing" her cell phone makes from her latest deposit receipt.

Before she opened her BETA account with Diamond Bank, Charles stashed her cash in a drawer or entrusted it to an informal collector who, as part of a traditional neighborhood savings program, kept a tally of vendors' savings in a little notebook.[1] Neither method was especially reliable or secure—Charles often feared the collector would run away with her money. Now, with Celestina and the BETA savings account, she watches her daughter's backpack bob on her way to school and plans for the future.

Access to financial services like bank accounts and digital payments can change the lives of women like Charles by allowing them to invest in their families' health and education, borrow to grow their businesses, and build a cushion to better manage emergencies.[2] Such access can improve women's earning potential, help them escape poverty, and reduce inequality across the globe.

Yet close to one billion women around the world have no access to savings, credit, or insurance, according to the World Bank's Global

---

This essay was originally published in *CNN Business*.

Findex report.[3] And even as the number of people opening bank accounts increases globally, the gap between male and female account holders in developing countries has stubbornly remained at 9 percentage points for nearly a decade. And that's the average: in Nigeria, 24 percent fewer women own bank accounts than men; in Bangladesh, it's 29 percent. But in India, the groundbreaking digital national identification system helped reduce the gender gap between account holders from 20 percent in 2014 to just 6 percent in 2017.[4]

Better access to financial services matters not just to women and their families but also to economies. With greater financial inclusion, women are better able to realize their economic potential, and the gains can be staggering.[5] The McKinsey Global Institute estimates that $12 trillion could be added to the global annual gross domestic product (GDP) by 2025 simply by leveling the playing field between women and men at work.[6]

Banks benefit, too, and more of them are recognizing that women are a promising and largely untapped client base that can fuel business growth.[7] Even low-income women save 10–15 percent of their earnings, and their balances do not fluctuate as much as men's—a consistency valued by banks.

The business case has convinced some banks to invest in products developed for and marketed to women. Since mobility and time constraints keep Amaka Charles and other Nigerian traders out of bank branches, Diamond Bank sends agents directly to the marketplace, using digital tools in place of traditional branch services. And because a recent central bank reform in Nigeria loosened account requirements, women can open an account without identification, signatures, or forms. Diamond Bank now has more female customers than ever before: nearly 40 percent of the six hundred thousand BETA clients are female, compared to 25 percent of its overall customers.

Vietnam's Maritime Bank hopes to have similar success with its new products. Recognizing that there are millions more Vietnamese women working in the labor force than have bank accounts, the bank developed new product bundles for different customer segments identified by the nonprofit Women's World Banking. These include home-based business owners who prize convenience, market traders who want access to loans and business training, and factory workers who want help managing their finances.[8]

The next financial inclusion frontier is in rural areas far from bank branches. As banks shift their gaze to the rural millions without savings accounts, a simple solution is already in customers' hands—their mobile phones. The potential gains are enormous: mobile money paid off in Kenya, where banks and telecommunications companies expanded rapidly to keep up with demand for mobile banking services while nearly two hundred thousand households were lifted out of poverty.[9]

In Tanzania, M-Pawa customers can open and use a Commercial Bank of Africa-affiliated account with just a cell phone and a registered Vodacom SIM card.[10] They find an agent (many double as shopkeepers) to deposit their cash or collect their microloan. Women with access to M-Pawa saved three times more money weekly than women with no access, according to a Center for Global Development study.[11] When access was combined with business training, they saved five times more money weekly and were more likely to open a second business, increasing their overall profits. They were also more likely to report feeling happy and empowered.

Access to a bank account is transforming women's lives and boosting economies from Nigeria to Tanzania to Vietnam. Close to a billion women around the world can, if given the chance—and the financial services—contribute to their families' prosperity and their countries' growth.

Banking on the Future: Moms Learn From Their Daughters

Gayle Tzemach Lemmon

Sometimes children are the best teachers.

That is the case when it comes to financial services for women in Tanzania. In the capital of Dar es Salam, NMB has been teaching students about why access to banking services matters. And these students, in turn, have been teaching their moms about the power of saving.

In Tanzania, where only 34 percent of women have bank accounts—compared with 45 percent of men—these students are making a difference.[1] Despite a narrowing of the gender financing gap in recent years, helped along by the rise of mobile banking, Tanzanian women continue to face structural, cultural, and regulatory barriers.

In interviews with three of these mothers at the Women's World Banking summit in Tanzania, it was clear the lessons had stuck. None of the women I met had received an education past primary school (Tanzania has only reached parity in primary school enrollment within the past two decades).[2] None had been raised by mothers who had bank accounts. All of them were deeply passionate about what they had learned.

"I wanted to save money for my daughter's future," said Asifa Shabas, whose oldest daughter, age twelve, taught her about bank accounts after she learned about them in school. "Before I was spending without a plan. Now I am planning and it is about saving money."

Other mothers agreed.

"I am a single parent and I want to save for my child's education," said Salma Mohamed. She, too, was encouraged to open a bank account

---

This essay was originally published on CFR.org. See Gayle Tzemach Lemmon, "Banking on the Future: Moms Learn From Their Daughters," *Women Around the World* (blog), December 8, 2017, http://cfr.org/blog/banking-future-moms-learn-their-daughters.

by her oldest daughter, now thirteen. "Saving money helps me send my kids to school, helps me to get medicine."

Mohamed says she only was able to go as far as primary school. For her daughter, she dreams of bigger.

"I want her to be a professional, a teacher or a doctor," Mohamed says. "I missed my chance at education and now I want my daughter to go to school."

None of the mothers I interviewed had a banking account before their daughters came home telling them about the program. They were intimidated by the idea of entering a posh lobby and talking to bank tellers. They also imagined that banks were only for people who could deposit hundreds of dollars at a time. Indeed, a World Bank analysis found that, worldwide, 57 percent of women without a bank account cited not having enough money as a barrier to opening an account.[3]

"I thought banks were for rich people, not for poor. Then my daughter insisted we should open an account," said Mariam Senge, the mother of two daughters, including a twelve-year-old in the program.

She remembers the first time she entered a bank.

"I wasn't confident at the beginning because I thought I was slowing down people who had more money," Senge said. "I was feeling so shy since it was my first time in a bank."

Since that first visit, she has gotten used to making her deposits.

"I have been able to manage money because when the money is at the bank I cannot spend it on things that aren't a priority," Senge said. "Little by little, I feel it will help us in the future."

PART II: ID LAW

Where Are the Women in Pakistan's Elections This Week?

Meighan Stone

Increasingly suspect and violent elections will determine Pakistan's new government on Wednesday. And from the candidate ballot to voting rolls, women are missing.

Despite the fact that women in Pakistan won the right to vote in national elections in 1956, the nation places dead last globally on women's participation in elections.[1] "Pakistan has a 12.5 million voter difference between men and women, a ridiculously high gender gap," says Lahore lawyer Saroop Ijaz of Human Rights Watch (HRW) Pakistan.[2] "One reason for that is the requirement for Computer National Identity Card (CNIC) to be eligible to vote." Even as traditional and religious barriers persist, it is lack of digital, legal identification that will keep most women from the polls this week—and prevent Pakistani women from achieving equality beyond election day.

NO CNIC, NO VOTES FOR WOMEN

More than 96 million residents and expat Pakistanis hold biometric, digital, and secure CNIC cards.[3] Issued at the age of 18 and required to access more than 336 services from the government, it is a must-have for modern economic life, from applying for a business loan to obtaining a driver's license—or voting.[4]

This essay was originally published on *Women in the World*. See Meighan Stone, "Where Are the Women in Pakistan's Elections This Week?," *Women in the World*, July 24, 2018, http://womenintheworld.com/2018/07/24/where-are-the-women-in-pakistans -elections-this-week.

"Despite the significant increase in number of CNICs issued to women over the years and the remarkable female voter turnout in the General Elections in 2013, the gender gap in voter registration is still increasing," says Aisha Mukhtar of UN Women Pakistan. "Mainly because a large number of women continue to remain deprived of their legal identity and cannot exercise their constitutional right to vote."

Discriminatory legal and cultural barriers make women less likely to have an official ID and shut them out of political and economic opportunity. Pakistan is one of only 11 countries where a woman must obtain national legal identification differently than a man.[5] A woman cannot apply without her marriage contract, permission from her husband, or his ID card. Without a CNIC, Pakistani women are technically barred from voting and other basic functions that men take for granted— leaving them unable to open a bank account, buy a plane ticket, start a business, or even purchase their own mobile phone due to Know Your Customer laws.[6]

Launched by the National Database and Registration Authority (NADRA) in 2000, Pakistan's ID efforts have largely been a success story in bringing identity into the digital age. NADRA's registration drives deployed women-driven recruitment vans, but faced numerous challenges, from warlords to unwilling husbands.[7]

"There are some places in Pakistan where women voters have been banned since independence and still can't vote due to [lack of an] identity card and local authorities who don't believe women should have a voice in elections," says Quratulain Fatima, a Pakistani Air Force veteran and policy expert on gender inclusive development. "Women lack access to the internet and have restrictions on their mobility. The government needs to fund more campaigns to register women where they are at, going to their homes to get them registered and political parties also have to do their part, if they want these women to be their voters."

CREATIVE IDENTITY POLICY: READY TO PAY MONTHLY FOR WOMEN'S EQUALITY

Instead of political party outreach, it was a safety net cash transfer program that drove a massive bump in CNIC enrollment for women in the poorest Pakistani communities. Launched in 2008 by the government of Pakistan with support from the World Bank, the Benazir Income Support Program (BISP) is a case study in how innovative identification policies can empower more women.

"The government's efforts have played a major role in incentivizing women's CNIC enrollment through economic empowerment schemes such as BISP, which makes CNIC possession a pre-requisite for beneficiary enrollment and subsequent access to stipend and services," says UN Women's Mukhtar.

Purpose-built by the government to boost enrollment of women, only a woman head of household with a CNIC could receive the monthly $15 BISP cash benefits.[8] It was an unmitigated success, helping drive a 94 percent increase in women obtaining CNIC and contributing to a total of 40 million women in Pakistan having CNIC within just four years.[9]

Bringing together BISP and CNIC also bolstered women's personal, economic and political agency. Women who received CNICs received more respect in their families, spoke up more about household matters, and, for the first time, felt economically empowered. Since women received the funds directly, some 64 percent of women recipients reported now having a voice in how money was spent, usually directing it to food, health, and education.[10] And political engagement was also an unexpected result of the program, with women wanting to know more about their rights as citizens and BISP participants even expressing they would vote more than those women who didn't participate.

WANT TO VOTE THIS WEEK? COME BACK IN 18 YEARS

The greatest barriers to women participating in this week's election could be bureaucracy and abject neglect. Pakistan's National Commission on the Status of Women recently estimated based on current CNIC processing times, it will take 18 years to close the voting gap between women and men voters. And Pakistani advocates agree that this election didn't bring the government outreach and education campaigns needed to ensure increased CNIC enrollment and register new women voters.[11]

"In the last elections, NADRA had mainstream media programs and advertisements to support women's voter registration, issuing national ID cards, and encouraging women to participate in the process," said lawyer and Digital Rights Pakistan Founder Nighat Dad. "This time around, we haven't seen such campaigns."

"The voting gender gap could have been much smaller, had the government been more active in reaching out to women to sign up for CNIC, that should have been done much earlier and been ongoing and constant," agreed Ijaz of HRW. "For the last two years, women's voting and participation has been part of the national conversation, but I don't think the benefits of those legal changes will be evident in this election."

LEGAL CHANGES THAT WORK: IF WOMEN DON'T VOTE, THE VOTE DOESN'T COUNT

Pakistani advocates agree that one way to increase the number of women both gaining legal identity and political representation would be changing election laws to increase the minimum threshold of women's participation. In October 2017, Pakistan passed an ambitious Elections Act, mandating that at least 10 percent of voters in each constituency must be women, or the results will be invalidated.[12]

"Why have they set such a low bar?" asked Dad, who has been actively monitoring women's engagement in the current elections. "It should be at least 25 percent and there should be punishment for people who don't allow women to vote. There are entire villages where women are not allowed to step outside their homes on election day in Khyber Pakhtunkhwa and southern Punjab."

Indeed, in 2008, not one vote was cast by a woman in 31 polling places in Punjab, despite being one of Pakistan's most progressive states for women's legal and economic rights.[13] But recent examples show legal reforms are working. In one of the first cases of the new law being applied, a local Upper Dir 2017 election in Khyber Pakhtunkhwa was invalidated. At the new election, women came out to vote for the first time in decades.[14] And in 2015, Fouzia Talib voted for the first time in her southern Punjab village, after a lifetime of being blocked by town tradition and "respect for our forefathers." She cast her vote with court-ordered police protection. As AFP recently reported, more women in her town are set to follow her lead this year.[15]

Dawn newspaper columnist and author Rafia Zakaraia sees cause for cautious optimism for women's political and economic empowerment in Pakistan's demographic trends. "When women come into urban areas and get economic opportunity, they increase the likelihood they will participate in the political process. There's increased awareness of the necessity of voting and that's your chance to have some modicum of influence on the political process. But even then, the independence with which they can do that is questionable."

In that fight for self-determination, legal identification is only the first step in Pakistani women's political and economic participation. Though Pakistan has made significant progress in registering women, remaining administrative, legal and cultural obstacles come at a high price. Keeping women out of formal financial systems and the voting booth robs the nation of crucial contributors to economic growth, and the voices of half its citizens.

How India's Controversial Biometric ID System Can Help Women

Gayle Tzemach Lemmon

The World Bank estimates that one in six people around the globe are unable to prove their identity—a burden that disproportionately affects women and girls.[1] Not only are women and girls confronted with structural barriers to obtaining official identification documents, ranging from restrictions on mobility to illiteracy, but many also face a significant legal hurdle. According to the World Bank's *Women, Business and the Law 2016* report, several nations require women to provide additional documentation such a birth certificate to even approach the government for an ID card, a condition that often ends the fight to be counted before it even begins.[2]

Life without ID compounds the barriers a woman faces in accessing credit, employment, healthcare and education for her children. Without proof of identity, women are often barred from accessing basic government and financial services, including cash transfers, pensions and educational scholarships.

Recently, new technologies have sought to transform the way people are counted, replacing traditional paper documentation with biometric data. Leading the path forward is India's Aadhaar system.

Launched in 2009, Aadhaar refers to a unique, randomly generated 12-digit ID number that's assigned to each of India's residents after they sign up. Aimed at boosting social and financial inclusion, registration

© 2017 Time Inc. All rights reserved. Reprinted from TIME.com and published with permission of Time Inc. Reproduction in any manner in any language in whole or in part without written permission is prohibited. See Gayle Tzemach Lemmon, "How India's Controversial Biometric ID System Can Help Women," *Time*, June 22, 2017, http://time.com/4828808/india-biometric-id-system-aadhaar-benefits-women.

is free of charge. The system uses fingerprints, iris scans and a facial photograph to verify an individual's identity. To date, approximately 94 percent of India's population has been enrolled in Aadhaar.[3] And, as a result, government benefits have reached their intended population more efficiently and more reliably, according to a 2017 report by the Groupe Spéciale Mobile Association, which represents mobile operators across the globe.

Aadhaar is also increasingly bringing India's unbanked into the nation's financial system. In 2013, the Reserve Bank of India mandated that Aadhaar be accepted as a form of ID when applying for a bank account. Subsequently, from 2013 to 2014, the number of bank accounts linked to Aadhaar increased from fewer than 2 million to 58 million.[4]

In 2014, Prime Minister Narendra Modi announced the National Mission for Financial Inclusion (Pradhan Mantri Jan-Dhan Yojana, or PMJDY), which seeks to provide all citizens with access to bank accounts, in part by allowing Aadhaar as an accepted form of ID. One study found that the rate of financial inclusion subsequently rose by 24 percent among women between 2014 and 2015.[5] Altogether, approximately 220 million accounts were opened under PMJDY by April 2016—the majority in poor, rural areas—suggesting that being able to use Aadhaar to open a bank account may be key to financial inclusion efforts.[6]

Despite the benefits Aadhaar offers regarding the ease with which an individual's identification can be known, security experts and activists have criticized the system as "the world's biggest surveillance engine."[7] They contend that increasing pressure on Indian citizens to enroll in Aadhaar (for example, an Aadhaar number is now needed to open a bank account and, increasingly, to receive public benefits) is a privacy breach.[8] Critics worry that storing demographic and biometric data in a central database poses a major risk to citizens if the database were to be hacked, or that it could be used by the government for ethnic identification or other purposes that are far less benign than the provision of government benefits.[9] Still, many international development professionals, including those at the World Bank, have hailed Aadhaar as a model for other countries.[10]

In addition to bolstering financial inclusion efforts, the ability of all citizens to obtain a national ID leads to a great deal of change for the better, especially when it comes to families' health and well-being.[11] Having a national ID can enable the tracking of vaccines and maternal care, facilitate school enrollment, solidify legal rights such as the rights to vote and to own property and can even prevent child marriage by providing evidence of a girl's minority status. In India, marriage of children under the age of 18 is illegal, but that has yet to stop the practice from happening.[12]

Ultimately, universal ID systems have the potential to contribute to a virtuous cycle of positive change for women's lives and families' prosperity. And counting women as part of the country's citizenry can help lead to a more prosperous and stable society—one where women can more easily access their nation's benefits, its healthcare, its education system and its banks.

PART III: LAND RIGHTS

A Place of Her Own: Women's Right to Land

Meighan Stone and Alexandra Bro

Last month, Liberian women activists marched to the presidential palace to protest the country's 2017 Land Rights Act.[1] Concerned for communities dependent on ancestral land for food and income, advocates called for President George Weah to ensure that legislation protects the rights of women and rural Liberians from privatization.[2] From inheritance practices to legal barriers to women owning land at all, Liberian women are not alone in their fight. Governments globally must reform land rights practices that harm women and hinder economic growth.

WHEN THE LAW SAYS NO TO WOMEN AND PROPERTY OWNERSHIP

When it comes to property ownership, women are not equal in the eyes of the law. According to the World Bank, close to 40 percent of the world's economies have at least one legal constraint on women's rights to property, limiting their ability to own, manage, and inherit land. Thirty-nine countries allow sons to inherit a larger proportion of assets than daughters and thirty-six economies do not have the same inheritance rights for widows as they do for widowers.[3]

These legal barriers contribute to a global gender gap in land ownership. An analysis of eight African countries found that women comprise

---

This essay was originally published on CFR.org. See Meighan Stone and Alexandra Bro, "A Place of Her Own: Women's Right to Land," *Women Around the World* (blog), May 21, 2018, http://cfr.org/blog/place-her-own-womens-right-land.

less than one-quarter of landholders.[4] In Latin America, the proportion of female landholders is about 20 percent, and in the Middle East and North Africa region, it is as low as 5 percent.[5] And even when women do control land, it is often smaller in size and of lower quality than that held by men. In countries like Bangladesh, Ecuador, and Pakistan, the average size of land holdings by male-headed households is twice that of households headed by women.

LAND LIFTS WOMEN AND THEIR FAMILIES OUT OF POVERTY

The right to land is about much more than the pride of ownership or a property title. A growing body of research confirms that women's lack of access to land not only hampers their economic prospects, but also has a profound effect on their families, communities, and countries.

A woman's income can increase up to 380 percent when she has a right to own and inherit property.[6] In Rwanda, women who own land are 12 percent more likely to take out loans to build businesses, and in India, secure land rights yield an 11 percent increase in women moving from subsistence farming to selling crops from their land.[7] Secure land rights for female farmers are also related to higher agricultural productivity and food security, important drivers of development.[8]

This economic stability afforded by land ownership in turn reduces women's vulnerability to domestic violence, poverty, and the impact of HIV/AIDS.[9] And the benefits to her family are significant, with her children 33 percent less likely to be severely underweight, 10 percent less likely to be unhealthy, and more likely to be educated.[10]

International legal and policy frameworks help set the stage for local change. In recent years, multilateral and global institutions have started to recognize the importance of strong property rights for development. Unlike the Millennium Development Goals, the Sustainable Development Goals reference access to land in its goals on poverty, hunger, and gender equality, and in 2016, the African Union formally pledged to ensure that women make up 30 percent of landowners by 2025.[11]

At the national level, many countries have successfully enacted progressive legislation to fight discrimination against women's land ownership.[12] In 2017, Nepal passed a Finance Act, which offers spouses discounted fees if they register their property jointly or in the woman's name.[13] Nepal also amended its constitution in 2007, and now grants sons and daughters equal rights to ancestral property without restrictions on marital status or age.

Recent studies show that updating national property regime structures can be another tool to benefit women.[14] In Ghana, which has a separate regime where each spouse can own and control their own property, women make up 38 percent of landowners. In Ecuador, which has a community regime where property is considered jointly owned regardless of which spouse bought it, more than half of all landowners are women. Automatic joint titling for spouses takes an opportunity for discrimination against women off the table entirely.

Lastly, at the local level, leaders must recognize that even with changes in legislation, cultural practices may not support women's land ownership. From work with traditional leaders to local land administration officials, legal reforms must be accompanied by adequate enforcement and community outreach to ensure that women and local communities are aware of the rights and benefits of women's land ownership.[15]

From inheriting land to a right to own her home, governments worldwide must change legal frameworks that discriminate against women. If the pathway to prosperity involves tackling the most entrenched social and economic barriers for women, it is a road worth taking. A nation's choice to leave land ownership to men alone is a sure plan for economic opportunity lost.

Reforming Women's Property Rights in Afghanistan

Gayle Tzemach Lemmon and Becky Allen

On paper, the law is clear: men and women enjoy equal property rights under Afghanistan's 2004 constitution. But on-the-ground reality says otherwise, as a combination of tradition and customary laws keep most Afghan women unaware of their land rights and far from owning property.[1] As the Afghan Ministry of Justice estimates, 90 percent of Afghans decide land rights according to customary laws—regulations developed and instituted at the regional and tribal level.[2] For this reason, few Afghan women are able to capitalize on their right to inherit and own property.

While customary law varies throughout the country, it typically pressures a woman to relinquish her share of an inheritance to her brothers in order to ensure her social protection in case of divorce, demonstrate family loyalty, and avoid discrimination and shame at the hands of her community.[3] The cultural expectation is that a woman's husband will become her economic provider and therefore she does not need her own land in her name.[4] According to this view, it simply makes more economic sense for a woman to leave her share of land to her brothers, who will use it to provide for their families while her own husband looks after her.

But this tradition ignores the good that comes from putting land in the hands of women. For one, with women's entrepreneurship on the

This essay was originally published on CFR.org. See Gayle Tzemach Lemmon and Becky Allen, "Reforming Women's Property Rights in Afghanistan," *Women Around the World* (blog), September 5, 2017, http://cfr.org/blog/reforming-womens-property -rights-afghanistan.

rise in Afghanistan, land could act as collateral for women who need credit to grow their businesses—and in the process create jobs and boost their family's income.[5] Second, owning land could help women working in agriculture increase their production rates by 20 to 30 percent, contributing to improved food security throughout the country.[6] And third, land ownership by women has been linked to reduced violence against women, with some experts estimating that a woman who owns land is up to eight times less likely to experience domestic violence, a scourge found all across Afghanistan and affecting nearly nine out of ten women.[7]

With evidence of the benefits of women's land ownership clear, the question is: how can the U.S. and Afghan governments, along with multilateral organizations, put laws on the books into action when the law is so often left in the hands of local tribal leaders?

The U.S. Agency for International Development (USAID) tried to tackle this question with the Land Reform in Afghanistan (LARA) project, which ran from 2011 to 2014.[8] The initiative established a Women's Land Rights Task Force comprised of prominent Afghan men and women as well as civil society to advise project leaders on land rights affecting Afghan women. The project proposed strategies for bolstering women's land rights, but it is unclear how much women's access to their land has changed since.

The U.S. Institute of Peace recommends addressing women's land rights within an Islamic law framework, especially given that the Quran and Hadith permit women to both own and inherit property.[9] As such, including local religious leaders in awareness raising campaigns and educational programming on women's land rights could boost buy-in from communities.

What is clear is that Afghan women face much more work ahead. As the most recent Afghanistan Demographic and Health Survey noted, only 17 percent of Afghan women independently own a house, compared with approximately 50 percent of Afghan men.[10] This issue is often seen as secondary to the conflict in the country and to the overall plight of Afghan women. But getting land rights right could help to address both the nation's stability and its prosperity. For all its citizens.

PART IV: WORKPLACE DISCRIMINATION

When Sexual Harassment Is Legal

Jody Heymann and Rachel Vogelstein

What do 424 million working-age women have in common? They all live in countries with no legal protections against sexual harassment at work.

Over the past few weeks, millions of women have shared their experiences with sexual harassment in the workplace, from Hollywood to Silicon Valley to state and federal legislatures.[1] Using the hashtag #MeToo, women recounted instances when they were subject to everything from demeaning comments to sexual assault, and denied promotions or opportunities when they objected to unwanted advances.

In the United States, where sexual harassment is legally prohibited, the #MeToo movement is giving rise to an overdue reckoning with workplace culture—and a newfound commitment to implementing laws already on the books. Since the movement began, prosecutors are increasingly investigating allegations of sexual assault, and numerous companies and professional associations have vowed to step up enforcement of their policies.[2] Importantly, the #MeToo campaign has gone global, inspiring women to share personal accounts of sexual harassment in 85 countries and counting, with women in France, Italy, and nations across Latin America and the Middle East launching their own offshoot hashtags.[3] In many parts of the world, however, sexual harassment is not only pervasive—it is also perfectly legal.

© 2017 Time Inc. All rights reserved. Reprinted from *Fortune* and published with permission of Time Inc. Reproduction in any manner in any language in whole or in part without written permission is prohibited. See Jody Heymann and Rachel Vogelstein, "Commentary: When Sexual Harassment Is Legal," *Fortune*, November 17, 2017, http://fortune.com/2017/11/17/sexual-harassment-legal-gaps.

According to a new research from the WORLD Policy Analysis Center at UCLA, 68 countries—more than one in three—do not have any workplace-specific protections against sexual harassment.[4] These legal gaps span countries in all regions and at all income levels, collectively leaving 424 million working-age women—including 235 million who are currently in the workforce—with no legal recourse when faced with an abusive supervisor or hostile work environment.

Many working women also remain unprotected against sex discrimination in other areas—including compensation, training, promotions, or demotions—which further jeopardizes their safety and status in the workplace. The absence of basic legal protections for women on the job creates the conditions in which abuse can thrive, since sexual harassment and assault are often presented as the price of admission for a job, raise, or promotion. For some women, impunity for discrimination in the workplace creates intolerable work environments. For others, it may deter entering the labor force altogether.

These consequences matter—and not just to women. Only around half of the world's working-age women participate in the labor force, compared to around three-quarters of their male counterparts, and sexual harassment and other discriminatory behavior that keeps women out of the workplace undermines economic growth.[5] One recent analysis from the McKinsey Global Institute estimates that closing gender gaps in the workplace could help add up to $12 trillion in global gross domestic product (GDP) by 2025.[6] For national economies, reaching gender parity in employment could boost gross GDP by 5 percent in the United States, 9 percent in Japan, 12 percent in the United Arab Emirates, 27 percent in India, and 34 percent in Egypt.[7] At a time when the global economy is still recovering from a downturn, we can't afford to ignore discriminatory conditions that reduce economic potential.

To reach all 2.4 billion working-age women worldwide, we need laws that prohibit sexual harassment and sex discrimination in the workplace in every nation in the world. And companies should take action in all of the countries in which they do business—not just those that already have strong laws.

To be sure, outlawing sexual harassment and sex discrimination is but one step on the road to workplace equality. After all, as the current outcry in the U.S. shows, federal and state laws prohibiting harassment went unenforced for decades in a range of sectors, from media to academia to the restaurant industry. And in many instances, even countries that already have laws on the books still need to strengthen those protections by closing legal loopholes that have enabled sexual harassment to go unaddressed or unreported, as lawmakers in at least two U.S. states have promised to do.[8]

But women and men around the world need more than a social media campaign to fight the epidemic of sexual harassment on the job. They need the legal tools that prohibit discrimination in the workplace, and provide a mechanism to hold perpetrators accountable. As courageous individuals continue to speak out, let's be sure to remember those who have the least protection against workplace abuses that have no place in the 21st century.

How to Benefit Women and Corporations Alike: Evidence From Nigeria

Jamille Bigio

A routine audit of a multinational manufacturing company in Nigeria found something wrong: women working on the production line at night. The company was penalized for breaking the law—in Nigeria, women cannot work overnight doing manual labor.[1]

The manufacturing managers felt under pressure to meet the company's diversity targets. At the same time, they wondered how they could promote a woman to be in charge of others if she had not been in the trenches with them, on the night shift, at some point in her career.

The law weighed against female candidates, reinforcing cultural beliefs that already discourage Nigerian women from pursuing manufacturing jobs. As a result, women remain underrepresented in the sector, and most occupy sales or administrative jobs. One Nigerian human resources director wondered why the country's laws would make it harder for women to work than men: "If companies can guarantee the safety of women in the workplace at night, what reason is there for the restriction?"

This is not just a question of fairness but of economics: a recent analysis estimates that Nigeria's gross domestic product (GDP) could grow by 23 percent by 2025 if women participated in the labor force at the same rate as men.[2] The International Monetary Fund suggested that Nigeria can make its vulnerable economy more stable by improving its low levels of gender equality (it ranks 122 among 144 countries on the World Economic Forum's global gender gap index).[3]

Companies benefit, too: according to the McKinsey Global Institute, greater gender diversity on executive teams is correlated with

---

This essay was originally published on *News Deeply*.

both profitability and value creation. They found that companies with more diverse workforces are more likely to perform better financially: they attract top talent, are more customer-oriented and have better decision-making processes. Companies gain even more when women executives are responsible for the core, revenue-generating part of the business—as opposed to support roles like human resources or information technology (IT) services.[4]

But for Nigeria's companies, the law impedes more female executives in core manufacturing roles. Until women have experience with all jobs on the production line, managers remain loath to promote them, and companies suffer for it.

The labor law that restricts women from working night shifts should be changed, as should several others. Nigerian women face significant obstacles to getting a job: they are unprotected from gender discrimination in employment and have no guarantee of equal pay for equal work. If sexually harassed in public places, women have few legal options. If women take maternity leave, they are not guaranteed an equivalent position when they return to work. On these barriers, Nigeria is not alone—according to a recent World Bank report, most countries still have laws that make it harder for women to work than men.[5]

Governments around the world are beginning to understand and limit the cost of inequality for women in the workplace. Over 110 countries in the past two years have reformed laws to improve women's economic opportunities. These changes have ranged from stronger sexual harassment laws in Afghanistan to increased maternity leave in Peru.[6] The Democratic Republic of Congo recently removed some of the same barriers that remain in Nigeria today, permitting women to work at night and prohibiting gender-based discrimination in hiring and promotions.

Companies should do more to promote legal reforms that increase women's economic participation; after all, this benefits women and corporations alike. Even in the absence of such reform, companies can better foster inclusion. The McKinsey Global Institute found that with committed leadership and thoughtful strategies, companies around the world have succeeded at improving the diversity of their workforces—and have profited from it.[7]

Nigerian companies are starting to understand the benefits of gender diversity. Some have instituted their own nondiscrimination policies, even though those are not legally required, and are fostering corporate cultures that—unlike Nigeria's society—encourage equal opportunities for women. Some have programs to groom the next generation of managers, and have ensured that half the participants are women. Such deliberate actions have translated to more women working in manufacturing than ever before, without compromising standards.

"Today, I see young women who are resilient," observed a Nigerian human resource director, "who want to break barriers and to do things that their parents didn't do"—from working the night shift on a production line to rising to the top of a company. Laws in Nigeria and around the world should enable, not impede, these opportunities, for the benefit of not just women and families but entire economies.

Nigeria can make its vulnerable economy more prosperous by reforming the laws that prevent women from fully contributing to society. Until then, it is in the hands of companies to lead the way.

PART V: FAMILY LAW AND WOMEN'S SOCIAL STATUS

Why Aren't There More Women in the Labor Force Across the Globe?

Gayle Tzemach Lemmon

Gallup and the International Labor Organization (ILO) recently released a landmark report on global attitudes toward women and work.[1]

Based on a study conducted across 142 countries and territories, the report finds that the majority of both men (66 percent) and women (70 percent) prefer that women participate in paid work.

These results hold true across the world, including in regions where women's labor force participation is notoriously low. For example, in Northern Africa, where the female labor force participation rate is only 23 percent, 79 percent of women and 57 percent of men believe that women should be allowed to work outside the home.

Globally, the results are correlated with age, marital status, geographic location and educational achievement. Perhaps not surprisingly, young women (ages 15 to 29) are more likely to prefer participating in paid work than their older peers, as are single women, women living in urban areas and women who have reached higher levels of education.

This leads to one question: if men and women largely agree that paid work is acceptable for a woman—and women want to work—why does the global female labor force participation rate continue to lag so very far behind that of men? According to the report, 76 percent of men and only 50 percent of women work globally—a 26 percent gap.

According to the study, men and women alike report managing the

© 2017 Time Inc. All rights reserved. Reprinted from TIME.com and published with permission of Time Inc. Reproduction in any manner in any language in whole or in part without written permission is prohibited. See Gayle Tzemach Lemmon, "Why Aren't There More Women in the Labor Force Across the Globe?," *Time*, May 17, 2017, http://time.com/4782443/female-labor-force-participation-rate.

responsibilities of work and family to be the greatest challenge facing working women, followed by the related issue of affordable childcare. While variations exist at the country and territory level, views do not differ significantly by region or level of development.

Separate research from the ILO suggests that paid family leave policies could help address this issue.[2] In particular, leave that is specifically earmarked for fathers encourages a more equal distribution of childcare and household chores. Flexible working arrangements and on-site or publicly funded quality childcare could further reduce the disproportionate burden of family and care responsibilities on working women.

In Brazil, for example, researchers established a causal relationship between childcare and female labor force participation: a study of more than 4,000 children concluded that increased access to government-funded childcare resulted in an increase in mothers' employment from 36 percent to 46 percent in less than one year.[3] Likewise, research exploring the expansion of after-school care in Chile suggests a positive correlation between publicly funded childcare and female labor force participation in the country.[4] This trend appears to hold true across regions, as similar correlations have been documented in an array of countries, including Sweden and Russia.[5]

The Gallup-ILO findings and related policy trends discussed here are significant not only to women, but also to households, communities and countries seeking economic growth in the global economy. Evidence indicates that women are more likely than their male counterparts to reinvest higher proportions of their income into the health and education of their children, creating a virtuous cycle in which families grow healthier and more stable over time.[6] Women are also less likely to partake in risky financial investments and more likely to make decisions that benefit the entire community.[7]

Ultimately, increasing women's labor force participation can drive sustainable economic growth and contribute to global poverty reduction. This is in our shared interest, as suffocated opportunity is the enemy of global prosperity and stability.

In the words of Gallup's Chairman and CEO Jim Clifton, "The world needs to advance gender equality and empower women at work. Not just for the benefit of women, but for the benefit of all humankind."[8]

Pakistan's Imran Khan Promises End to Discriminatory Laws

Meighan Stone

On Thursday Pakistan's Imran Khan declared victory to an uneasy nation reeling from election violence and vote tampering allegations, promising to address economic disparity and the rule of law. "We will set an example of how the law is the same for everyone," said Khan in his first televised post-election address. "If the West is ahead of us today, it is because their laws are not discriminatory. This will be our biggest guiding principle."[1]

Despite Khan's campaign statements disparaging working women and mothers, the policy platform released ahead of the election by his Pakistan Tehreek-e-Insaf (PTI) party specifically addressed gender parity, promising initiatives on women's education, economic opportunity, health care, and legal protection.[2] As it becomes increasingly certain that Khan will form a new coalition government, he has a powerful opportunity to deliver on his party's platform and further Pakistani women's workplace safety—and the economic growth of the entire nation.

WE MUST KEEP YOU WOMEN FROM WORK, BECAUSE US MEN ARE DANGEROUS

The World Economic Forum's 2017 Global Gender Gap report ranks Pakistan 143 out of 144 countries in the gender equality index, due to its abysmal performance in women's economic participation, political empowerment, and enrollment in higher education.[3]

This essay was originally published on CFR.org. See Meighan Stone, "Pakistan's Imran Khan Promises End to Discriminatory Laws," *Women Around the World* (blog), August 1, 2018, http://cfr.org/blog/pakistans-imran-khan-promises-end-discriminatory-laws.

Why aren't women in the office or university classroom? One reason is the near nonexistent enforcement of progressive laws to ensure their safety. In Pakistan there is no such thing as a safe space for women and girls—gender-based violence is prevalent both inside and outside the home. In schools and workplaces, women and girls face everything from groping to demands for sexual favors in exchange for promotions.[4] Even female legislators are not immune. In parliament women are routinely jeered at and criticized for their appearance.[5] And it's even harder for the many women outside Pakistan's metropolitan centers.

"Economically independent, empowered, and working women in small cities and rural areas are considered to have immoral character and are not given much respect in society due to religious debates on her role," says Noreen Naseer, a professor at Peshawar University, originally from the Federally Administered Tribal Areas (FATA). "Even if a woman works in an 'acceptable' job, she will face subtle forms of harassment, and if she chooses to enter a field that is traditionally male, such as politics, journalism, or activism, then she will face many challenges."

According to the World Bank, gender-based harassment and violence against women comes with a real cost to Pakistan's economic growth, contributing to only 22 percent of women participating in the workforce, compared to 46 percent of women globally.[6] A report released last month by the International Monetary Fund found that closing the gender gap in labor force participation could boost Pakistan's GDP by 30 percent.[7]

"There is a very strong link between gender-based harassment and women's economic empowerment in Pakistan," said lawyer and Digital Rights Pakistan founder Nighat Dad. "Men don't let women go work in offices or allow them to participate in the public space because of how other men will treat them. Men say 'for your protection, we cannot allow you to go work' in the offices of government departments, or practice as a lawyer or in the hospital as a doctor."

"The problem is Pakistani women are succeeding despite the system," says *Dawn* newspaper columnist and author Rafia Zakaraia. "The system continues to be extremely exclusionary and not particularly interested in making the workplace safe beyond these panaceas, like we're going to enforce the Islamic code of conduct and put women and men in separate sides of an office. When you put women in separate spaces, they wind up denied the best opportunities they are due. The answer is to give them recourse."

MAKING THE WORKPLACE SAFE THROUGH
THE POLICE STATION AND COURTROOM

Women advocates, lawyers, and lawmakers have won historic fights for new laws to reduce harassment of and violence against women, including a 2006 amendment to Pakistan's penal code on the protection of women, the 2010 Protection Against Harassment of Women at the Workplace Act, and the 2016 Prevention of Electronic Crimes Act (PECA), which criminalized cyber harassment.

Yet Pakistan still struggles to enforce laws that protect women against violence in the workplace and spaces critical to women progressing in leadership, like universities. Even where laws exist, justice is often miscarried in the face of "customary law." Pakistan's constitutional and formal court protections aren't implemented due to everything from fear of reprisal to traditional *jirgas* in tribal areas that issue judgments in ways unchanged since before independence.[8]

"Legislation has helped address serious issues related to gender-based violence and played a role of deterrence," said Naseer, whose own cousin was murdered in a FATA honor killing. "These are milestones in terms of lawmakers' commitment to ensure protection of women's rights, but have loopholes that fail to address the issue of gender-based violence in rural areas."

Women experience enforcement failures from the moment they come forward to report harassment and gender-based crimes to police. From interviews to medical examinations, police officers often don't have relevant training and even refuse to prioritize collecting evidence that can lead to prosecution.[9] Victims and their families face social stigma and rumors of past relationships can result in no punishment for perpetrators. As a result, many Pakistani women don't report crimes at all, withdraw complaints due to pressure from their family or community, or simply are unable to win their cases in a system that is rigged against them.

"There has been progressive legislation, spearheaded by women politicians at the provincial and federal levels, to deal with harassment and violence against women," said Lahore lawyer Saroop Ijaz of Human Rights Watch (HRW) Pakistan. "But there is a question of enforceability that should have happened really already. When the state has anti-women laws, it poisons the well."

THE PRICE OF PURSUING A LEGAL CAREER
CAN BE VIOLENCE

There are few cases that illustrate the challenges to Pakistani women who seek to pursue traditionally male careers than that of law student Khadija Siddiqi. Stabbed twenty-three times while picking her sister up from school by a male law school classmate whose advances she had declined, she refused to be silenced.[10] She pursued her case in court and used the press and social media to aid her campaign, with the hashtag #KhadijaTheFighter garnering nearly two million views.

Her attacker, the son of a prominent lawyer, was sentenced to seven years in prison but then acquitted in 2018 by a higher court. Siddiqi said her case showed the overwhelming "stigma against women in the justice system, in which the onus is on the woman to prove she is the victim."[11]

Without basic protection for their safety in higher learning and traditionally male career fields, Pakistani advocates say women won't be able to fully participate in professional workplaces and achieve economic agency. "When women do speak up about harassment, our courts and law enforcement do not support them," says Dad, "And then men say 'See, I told you, these spaces are not safe for you. You sit at home within the four walls of our house and then you are secure'. If women speak up, they will lose the freedom and liberation of work."

EXPANDING PROVINCIAL LAWS NATIONALLY
THAT PROTECT WORKING WOMEN

In addition to enforcing existing laws, Pakistan's new government can play a powerful role in women's workplace safety by encouraging all provincial governments to implement successful legal frameworks from other provinces.

On March 8, 2013, the Sindh Provincial Assembly celebrated International Women's Day by unanimously adopting the Domestic Violence (Prevention and Protection) Bill.[12] A coalition of civil society leaders, led by the Aurat Foundation, and female legislators campaigned for the act's passage for five years. The act articulates an inclusive definition of domestic violence that includes "economic abuse" for the first time, and established a prison sentence of up to two years for perpetrators.

And advocates achieved a big victory in Punjab in 2016, when their assembly addressed gaps in the Pakistani legal code through the passage of the Protection of Women Against Violence Act. Conservative religious organizations like the Council of Islamic Ideology alleged the laws were "un-Islamic" and "promulgated to accomplish the West's agenda to destroy the family system in Pakistan."[13] The act firmly established that violence against women is a criminal, and not a domestic or family, issue.

"Most previous drafts focused only on domestic violence, but I wanted to make sure that all types of violence came into play—sexual violence, cyber violence, economic abuse, psychological abuse," said Salman Sufi, director general at the Chief Minister's Strategic Reforms Unit of Punjab in a Council on Foreign Relations interview.[14] "In order to make women an effective force in the economic development of Pakistan, we have to make sure that first they are protected."

Instead of being turned away from police stations when reporting violence, the law gave women victims new provincial government support and protection through criminal punishments and civil remedies, from sentencing to legal and medical compensation to GPS monitoring of perpetrators.

OPPORTUNITY TO EXPAND ECONOMIC AND POLITICAL PROGRESS FOR WOMEN AND ALL OF PAKISTAN

Women in Pakistan achieved important milestones during election week, with reports of women voting for the first time since independence due to new legal protections and the nomination of Justice Syeda Tahira Safdar as the chief justice of the Balochistan High Court.[15]

From increasing the number of female police officers for investigation of gender-based violence to expanding the capacity of courts to address harassment and abuse, Pakistan's likely new prime minister already has a party platform of promises to deliver legal and economic empowerment for women.

As Khan said in his speech Thursday, "We have the second youngest population in the world . . . they need jobs." Let's hope that also means jobs for Pakistan's millions of talented women who are ready to work.

ENDNOTES

LET WOMEN WORK: THE ECONOMIC CASE FOR FEMINISM

1. Ben Hubbard, "Saudi Arabia Agrees to Let Women Drive," *New York Times*, September 26, 2017, http://nytimes.com/2017/09/26/world/middleeast/saudi-arabia -women-drive.html.

2. Angel Gurria, "Gender Dynamics: How Can Countries Close the Economic Gender Gap?" (prepared remarks, World Economic Forum Annual Meeting, Davos, Switzerland, January 25, 2013), http://oecd.org/economy /genderdynamicshowcancountriesclosetheeconomicgendergap.htm.

3. Jonathan Woetzel et al., *The Power of Parity: How Advancing Women's Equality Can Add $12 Trillion to Global Growth* (McKinsey Global Institute, September 2015), http://mckinsey.com/~/media/McKinsey/Featured%20Insights/Employment%20 and%20Growth/How%20advancing%20womens%20equality%20can%20add%20 12%20trillion%20to%20global%20growth/MGI%20Power%20of%20parity _Full%20report_September%202015.ashx.

4. Isobel Coleman, "The Payoff From Women's Rights," *Foreign Affairs* 83, no. 3 (May/June 2004): 80–95, http://foreignaffairs.com/articles/2004-05-01/payoff-womens-rights.

5. Bilal Y. Saab, "Can Mohamed bin Salman Reshape Saudi Arabia?," *Foreign Affairs*, January 5, 2017, http://foreignaffairs.com/articles/saudi-arabia/2017-01-05 /can-mohamed-bin-salman-reshape-saudi-arabia.

6. Devin Stewart, "Abenomics Meets Womenomics: Transforming the Japanese Workplace," *Foreign Affairs*, January 29, 2015, http://foreignaffairs.com/articles /northeast-asia/2015-01-29/abenomics-meets-womenomics.

7. World Bank, "Despite Progress, Laws Restricting Economic Opportunity for Women Are Widespread Globally, Says WBG Report," September 9, 2015, http://worldbank .org/en/news/press-release/2015/09/09/despite-progress-laws-restricting-economic -opportunity-for-women-are-widespread-globally-says-wbg-report.

8. UN Women, "G20 Leaders Launch Group to Promote Women's Economic Empowerment," September 8, 2015, http://unwomen.org/en/news/stories/2015/9/lakshmi-puri-attends-w20-launch.

9. Women Entrepreneurs Finance Initiative (website), http://we-fi.org.

10. Millennium Challenge Corporation, "The MCC Effect," http://mcc.gov/news-and-events/feature/mcc-effect.

11. Gayle Tzemach Lemmon and Rachel Vogelstein, *Building Inclusive Economies: How Women's Economic Advancement Promotes Sustainable Growth* (New York: Council on Foreign Relations, June 2017), http://cfr.org/inclusiveeconomies.

HOW A SIMPLE BANK ACCOUNT TRANSFORMS WOMEN'S LIVES

1. Jamille Bigio, interview with Diamond Bank customers and field agents, June 6, 2018; "BETA Savings Account," Diamond Bank, 2018, http://diamondbank.com/personal/financial-inclusion/beta.

2. Asli Demirguc-Kunt et al., *The Global Findex Database 2017: Measuring Financial Inclusion and the Fintech Revolution* (Washington, DC: World Bank, 2018), http://documents.worldbank.org/curated/en/332881525873182837/pdf/126033-PUB-PUBLIC-pubdate-4-19-2018.pdf.

3. World Bank, "Financial Inclusion on the Rise, But Gaps Remain, Global Findex Database Shows," press release, April 19, 2018, http://worldbank.org/en/news/press-release/2018/04/19/financial-inclusion-on-the-rise-but-gaps-remain-global-findex-database-shows.

4. Gayle Tzemach Lemmon, "How India's Controversial Biometric ID System Can Help Women," *Time*, June 22, 2017, http://time.com/4828808/india-biometric-id-system-aadhaar-benefits-women.

5. Corinne Delechat et al., "What Is Driving Women's Financial Inclusion Across Countries?" International Monetary Fund, March 5, 2018, http://imf.org/en/publications/wp/issues/2018/03/05/what-is-driving-womens-financial-inclusion-across-countries-45670.

6. Jonathan Woetzel et al., *The Power of Parity: How Advancing Women's Equality Can Add $12 Trillion to Global Growth* (McKinsey Global Institute, September 2015), http://mckinsey.com/~/media/McKinsey/Featured%20Insights/Employment%20and%20Growth/How%20advancing%20womens%20equality%20can%20add%2012%20trillion%20to%20global%20growth/MGI%20Power%20of%20parity_Full%20report_September%202015.ashx.

7. Mayra Buvinic and Tanvi Jaluka, "Mindful Saving: Exploring the Power of Savings for Women," Center for Global Development, March 22, 2018, http://cgdev.org/publication/mindful-saving-exploring-power-savings-women.

8. Women's World Banking, "Custom Product Bundles Can Deepen Financial Inclusion for Vietnam's Economically Active Women," August 20, 2018, http://womensworldbanking.org/news/blog/custom-product-bundles-can-deepen-financial-inclusion-for-vietnams-economically-active-women.

9. Tavneet Suri and William Jack, "The Long-Run Poverty and Gender Impacts of Mobile Money," *Science* 354, no. 6817 (December 2016): 1288–92, http://science.sciencemag.org/content/354/6317/1288.

10. "Welcome to M-Pawa," Vodacom, 2018, http://vodacom.co.tz/en/mpawa.

11. Buvinic and Jaluka, "Mindful Saving."

BANKING ON THE FUTURE: MOMS LEARN FROM THEIR DAUGHTERS

1. Asli Demirguc-Kunt et al., *The Global Findex Database 2017: Measuring Financial Inclusion and the Fintech Revolution* (Washington, DC: World Bank, 2018), http://documents.worldbank.org/curated/en/332881525873182837/pdf/126033-PUB-PUBLIC-pubdate-4-19-2018.pdf.

2. "Tanzania: Education Equity and Quality," UNICEF, http://unicef.org/tanzania/6911_10874.html.

3. Mariana Dahan and Lucia Hanmer, "The Identification for Development (ID4D) Agenda: Its Potential for Empowering Women and Girls," World Bank, 2015, http://openknowledge.worldbank.org/handle/10986/22795.

WHERE ARE THE WOMEN IN PAKISTAN'S ELECTIONS THIS WEEK?

1. Kelly Buchanan, "Women in History: Voting Rights," *In Custodia Legis: Law Librarians of Congress* (blog), March 3, 2015, http://blogs.loc.gov/law/2015/03/women-in-history-voting-rights; Quratulain Fatima, "Closing Pakistan's Electoral Gender Gap," *Jordan Times*, July 15, 2018, http://jordantimes.com/opinion/quratulain-fatima/closing-pakistans-electoral-gender-gap.

2. Election Commission of Pakistan, "Province/Area/District Wise Statistics of Registered Voters in Final Electoral Rolls 2018," 2018, http://ecp.gov.pk/Documents/generalelections2018/er2018/pdf/Summary.pdf.

3. Identification for Development, "Pakistan: Building Equality for Women on a Foundation of Identity," World Bank, http://id4d.worldbank.org/country-action/pakistan-building-equality-women-foundation-identity.

4. World Bank, *Technology Landscape for Digital Identification* (Washington, DC: World Bank Group, 2018), http://pubdocs.worldbank.org/en/199411519691370495/ID4DTechnologyLandscape.pdf.

5. "Pakistan," Women, Business and the Law, World Bank, 2018, http://wbl.worldbank .org/en/data/exploreeconomies/pakistan/2017.

6. Mariana Dahan and Lucia Hanmer, "The Identification for Development (ID4D) Agenda: Its Potential for Empowering Women and Girls," World Bank, 2015, http:// openknowledge.worldbank.org/handle/10986/22795; Rebecca Mann, "Banking on Change: Enabling Women's Access to Financial Services," Consultative Group to Assist the Poor, October 25, 2015, http://cgap.org/blog/banking-change-enabling -women%E2%80%99s-access-financial-services.

7. Identification for Development, *ID4D Country Diagnostic: Nigeria* (Washington, DC: World Bank, 2016), http://documents.worldbank.org/curated/en/136541489666581589 /pdf/113567-REPL-Nigeria-ID4D-Diagnostics-Web.pdf; Tariq Malik, "Technology in the Service of Development: The NADRA Story," Center for Global Development, November 5, 2014, https://www.cgdev.org/sites/default/files/CGD-Essay-Malik _NADRA-Story_0.pdf .

8. Tariq Malik, "Technology in the Service of Development."

9. Identification for Development, "Pakistan: Building Equality for Women on a Foundation of Identity."

10. World Bank, "Pakistan: Building Equality for Women on a Foundation of Identity," February 4, 2016, http://worldbank.org/en/news/feature/2016/02/04/pakistan -building-equality-for-women-on-a-foundation-of-identity.

11. Ghulam Dastageer and Rizwan Safdar, "Why Bans Persist on Women Voting Across Pakistan," *Herald*, July 3, 2018, http://herald.dawn.com/news/1154065.

12. National Assembly Secretariat of Pakistan, *The Elections Act*, 2017, Act No. XXXIII, Serial No. 118 (Islamabad: Gazette of Pakistan, 2017), 1435–561, http://senate .gov.pk/uploads/documents/1507114190_478.pdf.

13. Quratulain Fatima, "Closing Pakistan's Electoral Gender Gap."

14. Saroop Ijaz, "For First Time in Decades, Some Pakistani Women Vote: Authorities Should Promote Equal Participation in Elections," Human Rights Watch, April 3, 2018, http://hrw.org/news/2018/04/03/first-time-decades-some-pakistani-women -vote.

15. Yasir Majeed and Agence France-Presse, "One Woman Defied All Odds to Vote in 2015, Now More Are Looking to Follow Her Footsteps," Samaa TV, July 12, 2018, http://samaa.tv/news/2018/07/one-woman-defied-all-odds-to-vote-in-2015-now -more-are-looking-to-follow-her-footsteps.

HOW INDIA'S CONTROVERSIAL BIOMETRIC ID SYSTEM CAN HELP WOMEN

1. Identification for Development, "ID4D Data: Global Identification Challenge by the Numbers," World Bank, http://id4d.worldbank.org/global-dataset.

2. World Bank, *Women, Business and the Law 2018* (Washington, DC: World Bank, 2018), http://wbl.worldbank.org.

3. GSMA, "Aadhaar: Inclusive by Design; A Look at India's National Identity Programme and Its Role in the JAM Trinity," March 2017, http://gsma.com/mobilefordevelopment /wp-content/uploads/2017/03/gsma-aadhaar-report-270317.pdf.

4. Greg Chen, "India's Unique ID Could Generate Big Boost in Financial Access," Consultative Group to Assist the Poor, January 30, 2014, http://cgap.org/blog/indias -unique-id-could-be-about-generate-big-boost-access.

5. Nathaniel Kretchun, "More Women Are Financially Included in India Than Ever Before," *Wire*, October 21, 2016, http://thewire.in/banking/women-financially -included-indian-ever.

6. Anuj Srivas, "Twenty Crore Bank Accounts Opened: Where Does Jan Dhan Yojana Go From Here? An Explainer," *Wire*, May 3, 2016, http://thewire.in/banking/twenty-crore -bank-accounts-opened-where-does-jan-dhan-yojana-go-from-here-an-explainer.

7. Pranav Dixit, "India's National ID Program May Be Turning the Country Into a Surveillance State," *BuzzFeed News*, April 4, 2017, http://buzzfeednews.com/article /pranavdixit/one-id-to-rule-them-all-controversy-plagues-indias-aadhaar.

8. Rajeev Deshpande and Sidhartha, "Aadhaar Now Must for Government Schemes, Benefits," *Times of India*, September 15, 2016, http://timesofindia.indiatimes.com/india /Aadhaar-now-must-for-government-schemes-benefits/articleshow/54337574.cms.

9. Kevin P. Donovan and Carly Nyst, "Privacy for the Other 5 Billion," *Slate*, May 17, 2013, http://slate.com/articles/technology/future_tense/2013/05/aadhaar_and _other_developing_world_biometrics_programs_must_protect_users.html.

10. Jeanette Rodrigues, "India ID Program Wins World Bank Praise Despite 'Big Brother' Fears," Bloomberg, updated March 16, 2017, http://bloomberg.com/news /articles/2017-03-15/india-id-program-wins-world-bank-praise-amid-big-brother-fears.

11. Identification for Development, "ID4D Data."

12. "India," Girls Not Brides, accessed July 31, 2018, http://girlsnotbrides.org/child -marriage/india.

A PLACE OF HER OWN: WOMEN'S RIGHT TO LAND

1. Kevin Mwanza, "Liberians Plan Sit-In to Pressure Weah to Protect Land Rights," Reuters, April 26, 2018, http://reuters.com/article/us-liberia-landrights-law/liberians -plan-sit-in-to-pressure-weah-to-protect-land-rights-idUSKBN1HX33T.

2. Henry Karmo, "Liberia's Civil Society Petitions Legislature to Swiftly Pass Land Rights Law," Front Page Africa, April 20, 2018, http://frontpageafricaonline.com /news/2016news/liberia-s-civil-society-petitions-legislature-to-swiftly-pass-land -rights-law.

3. World Bank, *Women, Business and the Law 2018* (Washington, DC: World Bank, 2018), http://wbl.worldbank.org.

4. Cheryl Doss et al., "Gender Inequalities in Ownership and Control of Land in Africa: Myths Versus reality," IFPRI Discussion Paper 01308, International Food Policy Research Institute, December 2013, http://ifpri.org/publication/gender-inequalities -ownership-and-control-land-africa-myths-versus-reality.

5. "Gender and Land Rights Database," Food and Agriculture Organization, http:// fao.org/gender-landrights-database/data-map/statistics/en/?sta_id=982.

6. E3/Land, "Fact Sheet: Land Tenure and Women's Empowerment," USAID, December 1, 2016, http://land-links.org/issue-brief/fact-sheet-land-tenure-womens -empowerment.

7. Ibid.

8. Renee Giovarelli, Beatrice Wamalwa, and Leslie Hannay, "Land Tenure, Property Rights, and Gender: Challenges and Approaches for Strengthening Women's Land Tenure and Property Rights," USAID, August 16, 2013, http://land-links.org/issue -brief/land-tenure-property-rights-and-gender.

9. Vanya Slavchevska et al., "Beyond Ownership: Women's and Men's Land Rights in Sub-Saharan Africa" (working paper, World Bank's Annual Bank Conference on Africa, London, June 13–14, 2016), http://pubdocs.worldbank.org/en /170131495654694482/A2-ABCA-Slavcheska-et-al-2016-Beyond-ownership -working-paper.pdf.

10. Landesa, "Women's Land Rights," December 21, 2015, http://landesa.org/resources /womens-land-rights-and-the-sustainable-development-goals.

11. Susan Markham, "Why the African Union's Pledge to Advance Women's Land Rights Matters," Place, November 1, 2016, http://thisisplace.org/i/?id=a7fb5abc-627b-4874 -80b1-9e943f493487.

12. Chris Jochnick, "Women's Land Rights" (remarks), January 9, 2018, Council on Foreign Relations, transcript and audio, http://cfr.org/event/womens-land-rights.

13. World Bank, *Women, Business and the Law 2018*.

14. Ibid.

15. E3/Land, "Fact Sheet: Land Tenure and Women's Empowerment."

REFORMING WOMEN'S PROPERTY RIGHTS IN AFGHANISTAN

1. "Women and Property Rights," Canadian Women for Women in Afghanistan, accessed September 5, 2017, http://cw4wafghan.ca/sites/default/files/attachments /pages/cw4wafghan-womenspropertyrights-factsheet2_0.pdf.

2. "Country Profiles: Afghanistan," LandLinks, last updated May 2018, http://land-links .org/country-profile/afghanistan.

3. "Women and Property Rights," Canadian Women for Women in Afghanistan.

4. Elisa Scalise, "Women's Inheritance Rights to Land and Property in South Asia: A Study of Afghanistan, Bangladesh, India, Nepal, Pakistan, and Sri Lanka," Rural Development Institute, December 2009, http://landesa.org/wp-content/uploads/WJF -Womens-Inheritance-Six-South-Asian-Countries.FINAL_12-15-09.pdf.

5. Shaharzad Akbar and Taiba Pirzad, "Women's Access to Property in Afghanistan: Law, Enforcement, and Barriers," May 2011, http://harakat.af/pdf/research /977758d76a84de77b.pdf.

6. "Women in Agriculture: Closing the Gender Gap for Development," in *The State of Food and Agriculture*, Food and Agriculture Organization (Rome: Food and Agriculture Organization of the United Nations, 2011), 1–62, http://fao.org /docrep/013/i2050e/i2050e.pdf.

7. Landesa, "Women's Land Rights," December 21, 2015, http://landesa.org/resources /womens-land-rights-and-the-sustainable-development-goals.

8. "Afghanistan: Land Reform in Afghanistan," LandLinks, accessed September 5, 2017, http://land-links.org/project/land-reform-in-afghanistan.

9. Anastasiya Hozyainova, *Sharia and Women's Rights in Afghanistan* (Washington, DC: U.S. Institute of Peace, 2014), http://usip.org/sites/default/files/SR347-Sharia_and _Women%E2%80%99s_Rights_in_Afghanistan.pdf.

10. Central Statistics Organization, Ministry of Public Health, and ICF, *Afghanistan Demographic and Health Survey 2015* (Kabul, Afghanistan: Central Statistics Organization, 2017), http://dhsprogram.com/pubs/pdf/fr323/fr323.pdf.

WHEN SEXUAL HARASSMENT IS LEGAL

1. Andrea Park, "#MeToo Reaches 85 Countries With 1.7M Tweets," CBS News, October 24, 2017, http://cbsnews.com/news/metoo-reaches-85-countries-with-1-7 -million-tweets; Alyssa Newcomb, "#MeToo: Sexual Harassment Rallying Cry Hits Silicon Valley," NBC News, October 23, 2017, http://nbcnews.com/tech/tech-news /metoo-sexual-harassment-rallying-cry-hits-silicon-valley-n813271; Adam Nagourney and Jennifer Medina, "Women Denounce Harassment in California's Capital," *New York Times*, October 17, 2017, http://nytimes.com/2017/10/17/us/california -women-sexual-harassment-sacramento.html; Amy B. Wang, "Senators Say #MeToo: McCaskill, Others Share Their Stories of Sexual Harassment," *Washington Post*, October 21, 2017, http://washingtonpost.com/news/powerpost/wp/2017/10/21 /senators-say-metoo-mccaskill-others-share-their-stories-of-sexual-harassment.

2. "U.K. Police Investigate New Sexual Assault Claims Against Harvey Weinstein," CBS News, last updated October 31, 2017, http://cbsnews.com/news/harvey-weinstein -british-police-investigate-new-sexual-assault-claims.

3. Andrea Park, "#MeToo Reaches 85 Countries With 1.7M Tweets"; Sasha Lekach, "#MeToo Has Gone Global," Mashable, October 19, 2017, http://mashable.com/2017 /10/19/me-too-global-spread/#78AYyAUdSmqu.

4. WORLD Policy Analysis Center (website), http://worldpolicycenter.org.

5. International Labor Organization, *Women at Work: Trends 2016* (Geneva: International Labor Organization, 2016), http://ilo.org/wcmsp5/groups/public/---dgreports/---dcomm/---publ/documents/publication/wcms_457317.pdf.

6. Jonathan Woetzel et al., *The Power of Parity: How Advancing Women's Equality Can Add $12 Trillion to Global Growth* (McKinsey Global Institute, September 2015), http://mckinsey.com/~/media/McKinsey/Featured%20Insights/Employment%20and%20Growth/How%20advancing%20womens%20equality%20can%20add%2012%20trillion%20to%20global%20growth/MGI%20Power%20of%20parity_Full%20report_September%202015.ashx.

7. DeAnne Aguirre et al., "Empowering the Third Billion: Women and the World of Work in 2012," Booz and Company, 2012, http://strategyand.pwc.com/media/uploads/Strategyand_Empowering-the-Third-Billion_Full-Report.pdf.

8. Ricardo Lopez, "California Lawmaker Calls for Ban on Secret Settlements for Sexual Harassment," *Variety*, October 18, 2017, http://variety.com/2017/biz/news/bill-settlement-ban-sexual-harassment-harvey-weinstein-1202593778; Vanessa Friedman, "After Weinstein Scandal, a Plan to Protect Models," *New York Times*, October 23, 2017, http://nytimes.com/2017/10/23/fashion/sexual-harassment-law-models-new-york-state-harvey-weinstein.html.

HOW TO BENEFIT WOMEN AND CORPORATIONS ALIKE: EVIDENCE FROM NIGERIA

1. Nigeria, *Labour Act*, part III, §§ 55 (1–5), Laws of the Federation of Nigeria, vol. X, ch. 198 (1990), http://nigeria-law.org/LabourAct.htm.

2. Jonathan Woetzel et al., *The Power of Parity: How Advancing Women's Equality Can Add $12 Trillion to Global Growth* (McKinsey Global Institute, September 2015), http://mckinsey.com/~/media/McKinsey/Featured%20Insights/Employment%20and%20Growth/How%20advancing%20womens%20equality%20can%20add%2012%20trillion%20to%20global%20growth/MGI%20Power%20of%20parity_Full%20report_September%202015.ashx.

3. International Monetary Fund African Development, "Nigeria: 2018 Article IV Consultation; Press Release, Staff Report, and Statement by the Executive Director for Nigeria," March 7, 2018, http://imf.org/en/Publications/CR/Issues/2018/03/07/Nigeria-2018-Article-IV-Consultation-Press-Release-Staff-Report-and-Statement-by-the-45699; World Economic Forum, "Global Gender Gap Report: Performance by Region and Country," http://reports.weforum.org/global-gender-gap-report-2017/performance-by-region-and-country.

4. Vivian Hunt et al., *Delivering Through Diversity* (McKinsey Global Institute, January 2018), https://www.mckinsey.com/~/media/McKinsey/Business%20Functions/Organization/Our%20Insights/Delivering%20through%20diversity/Delivering-through-diversity_full-report.ashx.

5. World Bank, *Women, Business and the Law 2018* (Washington, DC: World Bank, 2018), http://wbl.worldbank.org.

6. Ibid.

7. Hunt et al., "Delivering Through Diversity."

WHY AREN'T THERE MORE WOMEN IN THE LABOR FORCE ACROSS THE GLOBE?

1. International Labor Organization and Gallup, *Towards a Better Future for Women and Work: Voices of Women and Men* (International Labor Organization and Gallup, 2017), http://ilo.org/wcmsp5/groups/public/---dgreports/---dcomm/---publ/documents/publication/wcms_546256.pdf.

2. "Maternity and Paternity at Work: Law and Practice Across the World," International Labor Organization, 2014, http://ilo.org/wcmsp5/groups/public/@dgreports/@dcomm/documents/publication/wcms_242617.pdf.

3. Ricardo Paes de Barros et al., "The Impact of Access to Free Childcare on Women's Labor Market Outcomes: Evidence from a Randomized Trial in Low-income Neighborhoods of Rio de Janeiro" (paper, World Bank Economists' Forum, March 2011), http://siteresources.worldbank.org/DEC/Resources/84797-1104597464088/598413-1302096012728/Pedro-Olinto_access_to_free_childcare.pdf.

4. Claudia Martínez A. and Marcela Perticara, "Childcare Effects on Maternal Employment: Evidence From Chile," Poverty Action Lab, August 2016, http://povertyactionlab.org/sites/default/files/publications/569_Childcare-Effects-on-Maternal-Employment_Chile_CLaudia_August2016.pdf.

5. Siv Gustafsson and Frank Stafford, "Child Care Subsidies and Labor Supply in Sweden," *Journal of Human Resources* 27, no. 1 (1992): 204–30, http://jstor.org/stable/pdf/145917.pdf; Michael M. Lokshin, "Effects of Child Care Prices on Women's Labor Force Participation in Russia," Policy Research Report on Gender and Development Working Paper Series 10, World Bank, April 2000, http://documents.worldbank.org/curated/en/550271468759014108/pdf/multi-page.pdf.

6. "Investing in Women and Girls: The Breakthrough Strategy for Achieving All the MDGs," Organization for Economic Cooperation and Development, 2010, http://oecd.org/dac/gender-development/45704694.pdf.

7. Gary Charness and Uri Gneezy, "Strong Evidence for Gender Differences in Investment," September 18, 2007, https://rady.ucsd.edu/docs/faculty/GneezyStrongEvidence.pdf; Ana Revenga and Sudhir Shetty, "Empowering Women Is Smart Economics." *Finance & Development*, 49, no. 1, March 2012, http://www.imf.org/external/pubs/ft/fandd/2012/03/revenga.htm.

8. "Most Women Prefer to Be Working and the Majority of Men Agree, ILO-Gallup Report Shows," International Labour Organization, March 8, 2017, http://www.ilo.org/global/about-the-ilo/newsroom/news/WCMS_545963/lang--en/index.htm.

PAKISTAN'S IMRAN KHAN PROMISES END TO DISCRIMINATORY LAWS

1. "Imran Khan's Speech in Full" (transcript), Al Jazeera, July 26, 2018, http://aljazeera.com/news/2018/07/imran-khan-speech-full-180726124850706.html.

2. Pakistan Tehreek-e-Insaf, "The Road to Naya Pakistan: PTI Manifesto 2018," 2018, http://scribd.com/document/383487528/PTI-Manifesto-Final-2018.

3. World Economic Forum, "Global Gender Gap Report 2017: Performance by Region and Country," http://reports.weforum.org/global-gender-gap-report-2017/performance-by-region-and-country.

4. Razeshta Sethna, Tooba Masood, and Ramsha Jahangir, "Misogyny in the Workplace: Hidden in Plain Sight," *Dawn*, updated April 19, 2018, http://dawn.com/news/1395215.

5. Sethna, Masood, and Jahangir, "Misogyny in the Workplace."

6. Uzma Quresh and Tanya D'Lima, "Addressing Violence Against Women in Pakistan: Time to Act Now," *End Poverty in South Asia* (blog), December 10, 2017, http://blogs.worldbank.org/endpovertyinsouthasia/addressing-violence-against-women-pakistan-time-act-now.

7. International Montary Fund, "How to Operationalize Gender Issues in Country Work," June 13, 2018, http://imf.org/en/Publications/Policy-Papers/Issues/2018/06/13/pp060118howto-note-on-gender.

8. Layla Quran, "In Pakistan, Abused Women Find Comfort and Justice at This All-Female-Run Center," *NewsHour*, PBS, February 9, 2018, http://pbs.org/newshour/world/in-pakistan-abused-women-find-comfort-and-justice-at-this-all-female-run-center.

9. Tahmina Rashid, "Ending Violence Against Women in Pakistan: Legislating for Cultural Change," Asia and the Pacific Society Policy Forum, February 7, 2018, http://policyforum.net/ending-violence-women-pakistan.

10. WITW, "Woman Who Was Stabbed 23 Times in Pakistan Speaks Out After Her Attacker Is Acquitted," *Women in the World*, June 12, 2018, http://womenintheworld.com/2018/06/12/woman-who-was-stabbed-23-times-in-pakistan-speaks-out-after-her-attacker-is-acquitted.

11. Alia Waheed, "Stab Victim Khadija Siddiqi: 'My Case Is a Fight for all Pakistani Women'," *Guardian*, June 10, 2018, http://theguardian.com/world/2018/jun/10/khadija-siddiqi-case-fight-all-pakistani-women-courts-stab-victim.

12. "Celebrating Milestones: With the Domestic Violence Act, the Hurly-Burly's Done, but the Battle Hasn't Been Won," *Express Tribune*, April 1, 2013, http://tribune.com.pk/story/529300/celebrating-milestones-with-the-domestic-violence-act-the-hurly-burlys-done-but-the-battle-hasnt-been-won.

13. Quran, "In Pakistan, Abused Women Find Comfort and Justice."

14. Salman Sharif, "Five Questions About Punjab's Protection of Women Against

Violence Bill," interview by Council on Foreign Relations, *Women Around the World* (blog), May 9, 2016, http://cfr.org/blog/five-questions-about-punjabs-protection -women-against-violence-bill.

15. "Women in Parts of Pakistan Vote for First Time Since Independence," *Economic Times*, July 25, 2018, http://economictimes.indiatimes.com/news/international /world-news/women-in-parts-of-pakistan-vote-for-first-time-since-independence /articleshow/65134897.cms.

ACKNOWLEDGMENTS

Many of the chapters in this volume have benefited from the input of colleagues in Nigeria, Pakistan, and Tanzania, who shared their time and expertise with the authors. We are grateful for their contributions; this collection has been enhanced considerably by their knowledge and generosity.

A special acknowledgment is extended to James M. Lindsay, CFR's senior vice president and director of studies, for his support for this project. We are grateful to Patricia Dorff, Erik Crouch, and Sumit Poudyal for their review of drafts and to Rebecca Turkington, Rebecca Hughes, Alexandra Bro, Becky Allen, Anne Connell, and Lucia Petty for their excellent assistance in the production of this collection and the chapters herein. Thanks also to Julie Hersh and Cayla Merrill for their help on production.

This collection was produced under the auspices of the Women and Foreign Policy program, and the compendium was made possible by the generous support of the Bill & Melinda Gates Foundation.

Rachel Vogelstein
October 2018

ABOUT THE AUTHORS

Becky Allen is an MBA candidate at the MIT Sloan School of Management. She previously served as a research associate for the Women and Foreign Policy program at the Council on Foreign Relations (CFR) and prior to that as the communications and development associate at the Washington Institute for Near East Policy. Her writings on women and economic development have been published by *Forbes*, *Fortune*, and Devex.

Jamille Bigio is a senior fellow in the Women and Foreign Policy program at CFR. In the Barack Obama administration, she served as director for human rights and gender on the White House National Security Council staff. From 2009 to 2013, she served as senior advisor to U.S. Ambassador-at-Large for Global Women's Issues Melanne Verveer at the Department of State. In addition, Bigio was detailed to the office of the undersecretary of defense for policy and to the U.S. Mission to the African Union. Bigio led the interagency launch of the U.S. National Action Plan on Women, Peace, and Security, an effort for which she was recognized with the State Department's Superior Honor Award and the Secretary of Defense Honor Award. Previously, at the United Nations, she worked to strengthen disaster management in Africa and the Middle East. She graduated from the University of Maryland and received her master's degree from the Harvard Kennedy School.

Alexandra Bro is a research associate for the Women and Foreign Policy program at CFR. Previously, she worked as a temporary program coordinator at Vital Voices Global Partnership and as an intern at the UN Development Program in Amman, Jordan. Bro holds a bachelor's degree in political science from Stockholm University and a master's degree in foreign service, with a concentration in global politics and security, from Georgetown University.

Jody Heymann is distinguished professor at the Luskin School of Public Affairs, Fielding School of Public Health, and Geffen School of Medicine at the University of California, Los Angeles (UCLA). She served as dean of UCLA's Fielding School of Public Health from 2013 to 2018. Previously, Heymann held a Canada research chair in global health and social policy at McGill University and was the founding director of the Institute for Health and Social Policy and the Project on Global Working Families. She also serves as founding director of the WORLD Policy Analysis Center. Heymann has authored and edited more than three hundred publications, including seventeen books. She has received numerous honors, including election to the U.S. National Academy of Medicine in 2013 and to the Canadian Academy of Health Sciences in 2012. Heymann received her MD, PhD, and MPP from Harvard University.

Gayle Tzemach Lemmon is a journalist and adjunct senior fellow in CFR's Women and Foreign Policy program. Lemmon is the *New York Times* best-selling author of *Ashley's War: The Untold Story of a Team of Women Soldiers on the Special Ops Battlefield* and *The Dressmaker of Khair Khana*. She previously led policy efforts and worked on the emerging markets team for the global investment firm PIMCO. Lemmon worked for nearly a decade as a journalist with the ABC News political unit and *This Week With George Stephanopoulos*. A former Fulbright scholar and Robert Bosch Foundation fellow, she serves on the boards of Mercy Corps and the International Center for Research on Women, and is a member of the Bretton Woods Committee. Lemmon received her bachelor's degree in journalism from the University of Missouri and her master's degree in business administration from Harvard Business School.

Meighan Stone is a senior fellow in CFR's Women and Foreign Policy program, focusing on women's economic empowerment, girls' education, and refugee policy. She previously served as entrepreneurship fellow at the Harvard Kennedy School's Shorenstein Center, where she researched refugee policy and collaborated with Harvard faculty to foster social innovation. As president of the Malala Fund from 2014 to 2017, Stone worked with founder and 2014 Nobel Peace

Prize laureate Malala Yousafzai to empower girls globally to learn and lead without fear. She has led high-level advocacy, international development, and media projects with Bono's ONE Campaign, the United Nations, Global Partnership for Education, World Food Program USA, World Economic Forum, FIFA World Cup, and Group of Seven summits. Stone serves as executive chairwoman of Pencils of Promise and on the boards of Congressman John Lewis's bipartisan Faith and Politics Institute, Indivisible, Civic Engagement Fund, Sweet Briar College, and the girls' coding initiative Kode With Klossy. She received her bachelor's degree from George Mason University and her master's degree in international social welfare policy from Columbia University, where she was a Congressional Black Caucus fellow.

Rachel Vogelstein is senior fellow and director of the Women and Foreign Policy program at CFR and professor of gender and U.S. foreign policy at Georgetown Law School. She is the author of *Ending Child Marriage* and coauthor of *How Women's Participation in Conflict Prevention and Resolution Advances U.S. Interests*. From 2009 to 2012, Vogelstein was director of policy and senior advisor in the Office of Global Women's Issues within the office of the U.S. secretary of state and served as a member of the White House Council on Women and Girls. Following her tenure in government, Vogelstein was the director of women's and girls' programs in the office of Hillary Rodham Clinton at the Clinton Foundation, where she oversaw the development of the No Ceilings initiative and provided guidance on domestic and global women's issues. An attorney by training, Vogelstein is a recipient of the State Department's Superior Honor Award and a National Association of Women Lawyers Award, and serves on the board of trustees of the National Child Research Center.

www.ingramcontent.com/pod-product-compliance
Lightning Source LLC
Chambersburg PA
CBHW071347290326
41933CB00041B/3043